INSTEAD
OF DYING

THE COLORADO PRIZE FOR POETRY

Strike Anywhere, by Dean Young
selected by Charles Simic, 1995

Summer Mystagogia, by Bruce Beasley
selected by Charles Wright, 1996

The Thicket Daybreak,
by Catherine Webster
selected by Jane Miller, 1997

Palma Cathedral, by Michael White
selected by Mark Strand, 1998

Popular Music, by Stephen Burt
selected by Jorie Graham, 1999

Design, by Sally Keith
selected by Allen Grossman, 2000

A Summer Evening, by Geoffrey Nutter
selected by Jorie Graham, 2001

Chemical Wedding, by Robyn Ewing
selected by Fanny Howe, 2002

Goldbeater's Skin, by G. C. Waldrep
selected by Donald Revell, 2003

Whethering, by Rusty Morrison
selected by Forrest Gander, 2004

Frayed escort, by Karen Garthe
selected by Cal Bedient, 2005

Carrier Wave, by Jaswinder Bolina
selected by Lyn Hejinian, 2006

Brenda Is in the Room and Other Poems,
by Craig Morgan Teicher
selected by Paul Hoover, 2007

One Sun Storm, by Endi Bogue Hartigan
selected by Martha Ronk, 2008

The Lesser Fields, by Rob Schlegel
selected by James Longenbach, 2009

Annulments, by Zach Savich
selected by Donald Revell, 2010

Scared Text, by Eric Baus
selected by Cole Swensen, 2011

Family System, by Jack Christian
selected by Elizabeth Willis, 2012

Intimacy, by Catherine Imbriglio
selected by Stephen Burt, 2013

Supplice, by T. Zachary Cotler
selected by Claudia Keelan, 2014

The Business, by Stephanie Lenox
selected by Laura Kasischke, 2015

Exit Theater, by Mike Lala
selected by Tyrone Williams, 2016

Instead of Dying, by Lauren Haldeman
selected by Susan Howe, 2017

INSTEAD
OF DYING

poems

LAUREN HALDEMAN

The Center for Literary Publishing
Colorado State University

For information about permission to reproduce
selections from this book, write to
The Center for Literary Publishing
attn: Permissions
9105 Campus Delivery
Colorado State University
Fort Collins, Colorado 80523-9105.

Printed in the United States of America.

Library of Congress Cataloging-in-Publication Data

Names: Haldeman, Lauren, author.
Title: Instead of dying : poems / Lauren Haldeman.
Description: Fort Collins, Colorado : The Center for Literary Publishing,
    Colorado State University, [2017] | "Colorado prize for poetry."
Identifiers: LCCN 2017033097 (print) | LCCN 2017034423 (ebook)
ISBN 9781885635648 (electronic) | ISBN 9781885635631 (pbk. : alk. paper)
Subjects: LCSH: Death—Poetry. | Grief—Poetry.
Classification: LCC PS3608.A54565 (ebook) | LCC PS3608.A54565 A6 2017 (print)
    | DDC 811/.6—DC23
LC record available at https://lccn.loc.gov/2017033097

The paper used in this book meets the minimum requirements of the
American National Standard for Information Sciences-Permanence of Paper
for Printed Library Materials, ANSI z39.48-1984.

For Ryan
For Dad

CONTENTS

ONE

Instead of dying, you move in with us. We fix the basement up with a shower & a small area for your bed & you come to live. I help you carry boxes down the stairs. We set up your record player. We hang up your old poster from 5th grade that says "Save the Wolves." Once a week, you make grilled cheese for us in the upstairs kitchen. Instead of dying, instead of being stabbed on the street in Denver, instead of bleeding to death surrounded by strangers neither you nor I will ever meet, instead of all that, you get a job at the local grocery store, stocking the shelves, watering the produce: collards, endive, grapefruit. Your face stays your face & your pain gets better & you swim at the Rec Center in the early light of spring & you are so not not not dead.

Instead of dying, they inject you with sunlight & you live. It is a highly experimental process developed in the deep caverns of Luray, where a fluid from the crevices of the previous earth is found to contain a slow conglomerate of sunlight. Scientists discover they can separate the plasma into a medicinal dose, a shot of which can bring a boy back from death after being stabbed three times in the chest. *The Belt of Orion,* they call it. And it works. The moment the needle goes into your arm, you open your eyes. The bright light enters your bloodstream. And we thank the doctors and the ambulance drivers and even the man who did this to you, since he provided us with the opportunity to infuse you with infinite illumination.

Instead of dying, you adopt one hundred cats and then you adopt one more cat and then you adopt the next cat. You adopt all the cats. At night, your apartment rattles with claws & fur. On the back of each cat, you place a small monitor to measure their purring and then you synchronize their purring. Knowing full well that cats dream our lives, you also synchronize their sleep. You amass them all into a bevy of knowing, coaxing their alpha waves into clear veins of telepathy. When they are asleep, it is high consciousness, the grandest meditation. When they are awake, it is mostly chaos.

Instead of dying, you are born first, instead of third; you are *firstborn,* instead of me, and you live the fragile first years of your micro-intense existence inside the complete attention of our parents, fully moored in the ballast of their parent-eyes, being the baby of the golden-squared carpet & the window rainstorm & the song sewn from the sound of your sleep. You wear the first clothes. You set the first standards. You become *that which would be compared to;* watching from a solid place of self as the rest of us scream into your house, our hands smaller than yours, our mouths like Yukon drafts, filling with the air of your fully formed words.

Instead of dying, you adopt all the cats and distill their purring into a liquid. This takes weeks under the camouflage canopy in a forest of Kentucky, coaxing the vibration up from monitors on their fur and into the copper tubing, until it condenses into almost crystallized wavelengths. The cats are very happy. Their purring creates a tincture that soothes internal organs: it sings each organ's specific music. It is a spirit that changes by constellation, although the FDA claims that this statement has not been evaluated. As though evaluation always determines worth.

Instead of dying, Easter Island. Instead of dying, the Upper Peninsula. Instead of dying, Mongolia. South Africa. Machu Picchu. Ireland. Huge fields in Ireland where you keep sheep that slowly grow our sweaters. Where you walk like an old man through the crystal forest of your coastline farm and brush the wood clean with warm water in a glass bowl. One sheep in the field looks up, but not at you. The sheep looks past you, through the trees, through the paper, at me. I write that the sheep looks up at me.

Instead of dying, you watch as I write *the sheep looks up at me.* We picture it, the sheep. Despite the distance between the told and the experienced, we come to an agreement. The sheep will stay the sheep, stuck in the cairn-strewn bramble of your forestry, but I must become the person imagining you dually: as my brother, living, watching me write *the sheep looks up at me,* and also as my brother, living, in the story where the sheep looks up at me. In the story, you are much older, moving like a wire with work-glove hands toward the said sheep. Your gray hair long, tucked in the back of your shirt. Each of these stories placed inside another story, making an infinite mirror of stories, making the actual story, the story we don't want, seem a little less real.

TWO

Which side of this room am I on? I am on the inside. Which side of this body am I on?

Days I accept the bed 1.
as a cold anchor. 2.
Days I accept the moving 3.
fur of the 4.
room. Days full of filth 5.
accepted. Days of gunk. Days like 6.
holding the Google 7.
Street Maps figure squirming 8.
over land, not letting 9.
it go. Days where I 10.
actually do this ^ at work: 11.
hold the Google Street Maps figure over the place 12.
where you died. I find 13.
the exact street in Denver and hold the little figure 14.
above it. I feel sick to be 15.
here, even just in Street View, but I do 16.
it because it 17.
seems like being close to you. Because 18.
a picture of this place is 19.
also a picture of you. 20.

14

1. I bed the accepting these days,
2. anchored cold, as a
3. moving acceptance. Days
4. in fur,
5. filthy and full; days rooming
6. with days, in the gunk of accepting.
7. I google the holding,
8. the squirming feeling: a figure mapped on the street
9. letting no land over
10. it. Where for days I go
11. to work like this ^ doing actual
12. pacing over your figure. Mapping streets, grueling, holding:
13. I find you where you died.
14. Your figure I hold; Denver floating in streets
15. above it; I feel sick to be
16. here, even just in Street View, but I do
17. it because
18. you are close to *being-like* here—it seems that
19. this place is the place I pick to pick
20. you up, pick you up, just so.

Maybe this spider loves me as 1.
much as my dog loves me 2.
but I don't recognize it in relation to 3.
my visual requirements. 4.
The dog's face is like 5.
my face, and the spider's isn't. 6.
What I am trying to say is 7.
maybe I should give this spider 8.
a chance. I allow it 9.
into our house, name it Bruce, 10.
let it live. Later, I call 11.
my senator & cry. My 12.
senator seems so distant 13.
these days. What is a 14.
relationship with a senator 15.
supposed to feel like? I am guessing 16.
not this. I don't even 17.
know what my senator does 18.
for me; I feel like I have 19.
to do everything myself. 20.

1. I loved a spider this May, I
2. loved a dog as much as
3. my relations, recognizing, didn't I,
4. that the requirements I visually
5. love are face-based, dog-based.
6. Isn't the spider's face my face?
7. Saying, trying to say: "Am I what
8. spiders give? Should I maybe
9. want this, allow this chance?"
10. Pursue him, name him myself,
11. call him *myself* later, live & let
12. me cry? My senator's
13. distance, it seems,
14. is a wet day. What is a
15. relationship with a senator
16. supposed feel like? I am guessing
17. *even?* Aren't I this, but not?
18. Does my senator know how not
19. to have an "I"-like feeling? No. "Me, for
20. myself, everything," my senator says.

What does a plant do 1.
with a photo? It catches 2.
up with it. We have 3.
to catch up with 4.
everything to see it. I am 5.
an old man trapped 6.
in a middle-aged woman's 7.
body: a middle- 8.
aged woman's body going 9.
at the speed of 10.
light. My body is 11.
the color of a specific 12.
prism of the universe; even 13.
this body, hunched 14.
now over this small 15.
internet of fire. If there 16.
were an online of 17.
the mind, I would go there & 18.
make an order 19.
for the most incredible gentleness. 20.

1. Do plants know what
2. catches them? Photos with
3. *having-us* get put up
4. without catching us.
5. Am I it that sees everything?
6. An old man trapped
7. in a middle-aged woman's
8. middle body;
9. going as a body into a woman's age.
10. Of speed, the adage:
11. my body is light.
12. Specific colors of the
13. universe; prisms
14. hunched inside this body:
15. this small oven.
16. Fire of the internet.
17. Online is a
18. *there,* and go do I, minding the
19. order, making
20. credible all that is gentle.

Temperature is a product 1.
of being embodied. 2.
It is a measurement that exists 3.
only because of objects. 4.
It is a comfortable old hurt: 5.
the return of a radar blip, like how 6.
I leave a voicemail 7.
on my dead brother's phone. 8.
How I text my dead brother 9.
"I miss you" 10.
then delete it. What makes me 11.
do this? It is not a good idea. 12.
I feel weird for 13.
whole days afterwards. 14.
Then the feeling turns into 15.
another feeling and I forget. 16.
Only this poem makes 17.
me remember. 18.
What a great poem. 19.
Thanks, poem. 20.

1. Produce a temperature
2. body, and be.
3. Exit that measurement, and become
4. an object. Because only
5. hurt holds comfort. Is it
6. a blip or the radar's return of a blip?
7. Mail me his voice leaving.
8. Phone my brother's deadness to me.
9. I'm texting my dead brother
10. "I miss you":
11. I make what it deletes.
12. The idea of god is not a doing. This
13. weird feeling,
14. warding away days, whole
15. intuition of feeling, then
16. forgetting. Feeling another one
17. made this poem, this one *only*
18. remembers. So my
19. poem is great, but what
20. help is it, verily?

Yes. Alien life-forms exist 1.
& they are human consciousness. 2.
Yes, alien 3.
life-forms exist & 4.
they are your thoughts. 5.
Yes, alien life- 6.
forms exist & are 7.
your thoughts & therefore 8.
go undetected. The 9.
best way to survive 10.
on an alien planet 11.
is to go undetected or convince 12.
the current inhabitants you're 13.
one of them. Are you 14.
your thoughts? Do you 15.
feel separate from your thoughts? 16.
Do any other animals 17.
make plastic thermoses? 18.
"This is *ridiculous*," say my thoughts. 19.
"Quit looking at us. Just quit it." 20.

1. Existing forms of life are alien; yes &
2. conscious of humans, they are.
3. Alien, yes:
4. as existing forms your life
5. into thoughts, you are the
6. life of illusion. Yes, you
7. are existing in form &
8. therefore in thought, you
9. think you detect each thought as new;
10. surviving the way best
11. for this planet. Alien,
12. convincing the detective to go is to
13. argue with inhabitants. Currently
14. you are them: once
15. you do their thoughts
16. they think you aren't separate. Feel
17. the animals, are there any that do
18. thoroughly miss plastic? Make
19. their thoughts ridiculous. Make them
20. sit looking & be quiet.

THREE

Hatching out of an egg was hard

A lot of rainbows came to me, and they hugged me

The flashlight kept getting into the woods, and it shot out a feather and a ball

Can you put a million minutes on the timer?

The prisms are making themselves

My hand is colors

The snow glitters are glowing

No one gets old in *this* house

Did the bubbles run out of batteries?

Is the internet box invisible?

How many dinosaurs is *a diamond of dinosaurs?*

What is the opposite of suffering—
The prism, or the prism's light?

My skin smells like the sun
after I've been in the sun

That rainbow spelled seven days, the one that was floating

I love you for my life, for the day and night

I love you for my life

I'm going to wear a cough today

The cough will be printed on my shirt

I'm going to feel some old gravity today

I'm going to tell on myself

Maybe we need a new lamp since this lamp's ripples are standing up strange

Maybe those prisms are our wishes that we made when we came back from our moonwalk

Maybe we can catch water with a square & then the water can cool down & become fish

Maybe we can carry the water in our ears as we walk

How about when I was nine I married a panda?

How about my first word was *mine?*

How about we give these stones a bath in hot soil?

How about I turn into an electromagnet?

How about you

How about you

How about you listen to me as proof of me?

I had a dream last night that my body spoke to me!
But all it said was "drink more water"

Black holes are where the milk valley dies

The floor is stuck—it needs to let the rainbow in

Before the thinking is the knowing
The thinking is added to the knowing

FOUR

Ptolemy

Did you see that? That was Saturn

Loops a cyclical / crystalline path
Saturn chimes / a finished halo

Hangs the world / upon the earth-nothing
Saturn a tone / of the looping halo

Makes a precise / spirograph   spiral
Saturn a candle crowned by a web

Did you see that? That was Saturn.
That / was Saturn. That / was Saturn.

Aristotle

Crystalline epicycles predict your future behavior so it is super important

The crystalline spheres under the control of charts

The charts crystalline charts / The hands crystalline hands

All human behavior is set in crystalline cycles so it is super important

Crystalline spheres of unmoving stars

Past the moon is perfection / Past the moon is fixed

Past the moon there's a statue looking down with no pupils

A floating head projection

A super important floating head

Nicolaus Copernicus

Let us say the sun. Quiet.
Quiet. Let us whisper

the sun. Secret. Hid.
Concerning the orbs /

The whole revolution /
Let us bypass the fact

it's completely insane.
So take up your palm

and move the sun.
Move it to the center instead.

What does it mean?
Now *we* are turning

Lonely and neutral /
We are turning instead.

Tycho Brahe

The gold on his face / tap the gold on his face
An eyeball beam shooting up / out of a castle

He builds metal eyes / He gets everything
Gets a castle of eyeballs / built onto an island

Call the clairvoyant helper / the mercurial nose
Call the eyeball growing long / inside the dark hallway

Only Kepler is allowed / into this closeness
Kepler brushing the soft metal nose

Pull the camera away now / from their tiny dark notebooks
Pull the camera back slowly / through the window of stone

Johannes Kepler

Tender his notes / into the brightness
Math shining through / the manuscript's lace

See the long etched mane / on the immobile circle
See the floating ellipses / around the flambeau

The math does not know / about all the stories
Math does not think / the papacy thinks

Inside the math now is a whole power
Neon ellipses formed out of the air

Inside the math now is a base power
Powerful because it can wait

Galileo Galilei

My daughter's ear is listening somewhere.
How the sun is the center and /

What is another word for the center?
Surrounded.

The opposite is / we're on the outs.

I've moved the earth from the prized position.
(I didn't move it—no—it was already there)
They are angry / They're angry / They are so angry

They scared / the idea
of themselves now feeling the death

Blind / Trapped / Old / Out

My daughter. My daughter. She was the only
one

Yes, listener, I am still telling the truth
but I'm telling it less.

Isaac Newton

Archival his archrival
dynamic celestial mechanics

masses of planets, tides
the equatorial bulge

Say there is an inward force / another type of power

Inside the apple, it sees us / as rising.

Mother, I feel / what? / The hug of the world
Gigantic swirling vortex of invisible matter

NATURE & nature's laws / lit up with watching
Watching the apple inside of its twirl

Eighth Heaven

Inside a black hole / what is it like?

17th-century gravity / quiet quiet
Stars sphere each other / a bear's throat

Black holes the hand holds / lightning lightning
The municipal clerk with a wondrous throat

Bearded fortune teller / we set a timer
Aging sun of calm / in our eight throats

What is it like / inside a black hole? Look around

FIVE

*On am I, on I am. Rooming with this side, which
is that side, which is inside. The
on that I am is a body.*

NASA told us about the 1.
stepmother's tongue, the snake plant: 2.
how it gives out oxygen at night, 3.
drinks in carbon monoxide by day, 4.
weaving molecules of humanity 5.
through the anti-gravity. 6.
When I looked down from 7.
myself, it was all point 8.
perspective. Because I didn't 9.
know which way was up, you 10.
became up, you seemed 11.
to embody *up*. Moving up towards 12.
what I thought was you. Never 13.
has an object been so much 14.
like a fist of thrones, a thirst 15.
of ferns, a first thorn 16.
of many thorns—your 17.
body growing out & away 18.
from the place I thought we 19.
were traveling to, together. 20.

1. About us: We told NASA
2. to plant a snake, tongue a moth, step
3. night into oxygen, give it out
4. day by day beside monoxide & carbonation.
5. Human molecules were weaving
6. gravity through
7. our born-nook. When we
8. pointed ourselves out, all was ourselves:
9. didn't we become perspective?
10. You were the only one who knew.
11. Suddenly you became
12. two words: un-moving / un-embodied. *Or*
13. *Never-you. Or Was-thought.* What I
14. must have been objecting to
15. first, and fast, like
16. the learned worst-of-things
17. about your torn hands,
18. was the way our bodies disappeared
19. from the place I thought we
20. were traveling to together.

Sometimes the voices 1.
of those we love 2.
disgust us. I love you desperately 3.
now leave me alone. 4.
You say "When you grow smaller 5.
I will be your mommy." Maybe. 6.
Our research has shown that our 7.
research doesn't matter. 8.
What size are our senses? Your body 9.
is small, but your senses 10.
are the same size as mine. 11.
When you sleep sometimes 12.
I stare you back 13.
into my womb. 14.
Let me be alone 15.
with this checking account. Let me 16.
figure this checking account 17.
out. I'm thinking 18.
about money; feeling money the way 19.
you feel saliva in your mouth. 20.

1. Voices sometimes
2. love us, those of
3. the desperate, of love, but I disgust
4. alone myself. You leave now
5. smaller than when you were growing up. Say you
6. maybe are a mommy: will I
7. show you research of our
8. matter? Doesn't our research-
9. body sense our size? What
10. senses are but small:
11. mine. If size is the same,
12. sometimes we sleep *as you*. When
13. I stare you back
14. into my womb,
15. we are alone, letting
16. me tell our account. Checking this with
17. our account, checking your figure
18. that thinks "I'm out."
19. The way money feels is only about money:
20. like mouthing your saliva to feel yourself.

I was so tired, even 1.
my cobwebs were dizzy. 2.
Lying down was the only drug 3.
I had left. I put a 4.
candle inside of a paper 5.
lamp & tried to describe death 6.
to a child. Longed for a friend long 7.
ago estranged. These 8.
landscapes filled with 9.
the necessities to leave them: 10.
gas stations, bus stops, 11.
electrical wire 12.
over an irritation of field. 13.
I meant to miss one person 14.
a day, but instead missed 15.
everyone all at once. Dear mutt on 16.
the porch, release us. We've 17.
been the dream 18.
you kick for so long & 19.
now we too are gone. 20.

1. Even as tired as I was
2. dizzy, where cobwebs
3. drug only me down, I was lying
4. a bit. I had, with
5. paper wicks inside a candle,
6. dead-described the lamp,
7. long-texted my friend, my child.
8. These estranged egos,
9. filled with landscapes,
10. leave the necessities.
11. *Stop the bus, rest the gas,*
12. *wire for electrical*
13. *fields.* Over-irritated,
14. I meant to miss one person
15. a day, but instead missed
16. everyone all at once. Dear mutt
17. that we've released: the porch that
18. makes the dream bend is
19. longing for sleep, kicking, so
20. gone, too, for the now.

There is a fury of space   1.
and then more space out in space,   2.
then there is,   3.
okay, even more   4.
space after that. There is a flurry   5.
of "myself" inside   6.
the space, followed   7.
by light years of matter. Dark   8.
home of my brain, dear   9.
skull, bone and   10.
bullshit: don't follow   11.
the live wire of the   12.
internet today. May the   13.
GIFs stop twirling   14.
their kitten tails,   15.
inside the open unseen pages of   16.
the world. There is a puff   17.
of panic & a void   18.
filled with worry: a flurry of me   19.
surrounded by the opposite of everything.   20.

1.   There is a fury of space
2.   and then more space out in space
3.   —an O is there; space of
4.   more evenness is there.
5.   A flurry of "is" is there. After space:
6.   inside myself. And
7.   following space: the
8.   dark matter of years, the light
9.   a deer brings into my house.
10. Bone-skull that I am,
11. I keep following the shifting, bold
12. wire of living—I say
13. "MAYDAY!" when the internet
14. twirls to a stop. Yet myths
15. tell of kittens, their
16. pages seen unopened, inside
17. puffs of the world. How this
18. void of panic
19. in me is a flurry—a worry-less fill—
20. a thinking every opposite surrounds itself with.

Unperceived magic bursts 1.
forth. You ask, you tap on 2.
the crystal in your skull. 3.
The beam of light only shows when you 4.
let go of the beam, 5.
creating the least amount of 6.
suffering. I couldn't keep 7.
up with my online store's orders 8.
& this caused suffering. 9.
So I meant to change my 10.
ways. I tapped the crystal 11.
in my skull & waited, 12.
saying please, saying help, saying 13.
"If I don't believe 14.
in a specific name for god, 15.
can an unspecifically named 16.
god help me?" Does the 17.
belief part apply to the name 18.
or the idea? How granular 19.
are the specifics? 20.

1. Burst of magic perceived
2. on tap: you ask yourself forth.
3. Skull, you are a crystal
4. when you show only light, beaming
5. light, beaming goblet
6. of mountains, lest the creating.
7. Keep my suffering
8. ordered, store a line on
9. suffering. Call this
10. my change, mean that I
11. crystallize & tap ways
12. for waiting. Skull me my
13. thanks-saying, my help-saying, please.
14. "If you don't believe
15. in a specific name for a god,
16. naming unspecifically can
17. do you help." *God,*
18. the name, applies partly to belief,
19. granular as ideas: as
20. specific as the beings that are believing.

SIX

They got out of the harbor just in time, but they couldn't get out of their minds

Teachers pinning certificates of participation on the gravestones

When your head hurts, your head falls asleep

May all beings be free of suffering
including me, including me

Waiting is the way the cake and candles arrive

Time is an illusion, but only an adult writes that down

I want a heart cake for my birthday & I want to eat it in the basement with my friends so we can watch the cat meow

With this world, we are enchanted

The spell of the world pouring down

What does the night taste like?
It tastes like candy hearts

Hello, I'm Princess Twilight:
the princess of doctor's appointments

Today at recess, the wind sang a boring song,
a really boring song

Only kids who have my name can see what I see

This tree is happy and this tree is frustrated

Right now I need to get my eyebrows mad so I can talk to these trees

Maybe we can get a Band-Aid for them to get their madness away

I want to feel their madness away with this machine

Let's give those dogs a treat of bones

Now come see what I'm throwing out

There is a beaver hiding in that pail of trees

Morning is the afternoon of the night

You have to pay attention or else you'll lose it

Here's a good blanket—this one *doesn't* have cat pee on it

The wrong tube goes to the coffers, the right tube goes to the belly

I'm a ballerina with bones

It tastes like all the colors that are on the box

Usually kites come down on their own

Nostalgia only works if you are able to go back

But I don't *want to* share with myself

Kitty is climbing that great ladder of shadows

It's a better charm when you use the ramp

If I had some of those treats I could eat some of those treats

But what should I do when the hurting is coming?

That marching band was so busy

This grape is waiting for its turn in my mouth

That M has so many points

This chicken belongs to a sports team

That light can summon clouds inside of it

This music sounds like good napping music

That clock is moving through birds

This is a song, not a choice

E: One time I was eating my lunch. (silence)
L: And?
E: And what?
L: Is that the whole story?
E: Yes . . . That is the only story I have.

*

L: What's that face?
E: It's a mad face of no scissors.

*

E: There's a show about the sun and the moon.
L: Oh really? What's that show called?
E: It's called *Space*.

*

L: I love you.
E: Me neither.

*

E: What's that?
L: That's a place of worship.
E: Oh. Is that where we go to make our wish?

*

What are you writing about, the kid asks.
You. I'm writing about you, I say.

SEVEN

Instead of dying, your friend fixes you up with a job in Sault Ste. Marie, finishing tax documents in a small office, looking out at the slight 21-ft. sea change between Lake Michigan and Lake Huron. You hire your niece to manage the incoming and outgoing mail ships. There is a bright spot on the map just south of town, where the lake and the shore cannot be drawn, and that is where you go when the hurting is coming.

Instead of dying, we take you in—sick, alone, confused —and start a series of healing regimens. For the first week you drink only water infused with lavender and vinegar. After the new moon, we begin to feed you base elements: cream of tartar, kombucha, filmjölk, carrots. When the visions subside, we start the physical routine. The air is still cold as we start your lake swimming cycles—twice across & back the length. You hear robins like ticker tape through the branches of April. Your mood improves. We cut out bread, cereals, muffins, milk. We cut out gumdrops, taffy, milkshakes, wheat. Your hair calms down, your fingernails are trimmed. Instead of dying, you start jogging, in a zip-up tracksuit, early in the morning, sunlight a disco ball across your face, lawn sprinklers starting up all over the neighborhood.

Instead of dying, you build an elaborate village out of plumbing. Even the plumbing has plumbing. You tell the community that this construct of vital passageways is indicative of microcosms within the geodesic loop. You tell them that space isn't space without unfilled vessels. You explain how the pipes are not the actual substance of the village's construction—it's the air that the tubes go through. "Ignore the pipes," you say. "The real plumbing is the space in-between." This is the true disposal system. This was the way the universe is flushed & refilled.

Instead of dying, you study marine biology at 2,475 fathoms deep in the Mariana Trench. One evening you discover the effects of Chlorophyta algae on the mitochondria of single-cell amoebas, and, making a cognitive leap, realize the relationship to a similar function in the human neocortex. This discovery leads to the creation of *The Belt of Orion,* a mission that spearheads synchronizing the complex mastery of seafrond supplementation, sweeping the field of neurobiological research, with a focus on the regeneration of the myelin insulating sheath around the axon of specifically targeted nerves. And suddenly people in memory-units all around the nation are recognizing the faces of loved ones; they are dancing the two-step beside transistor radios; they are doing crosswords again with blue pens in the soaring nursing home atrium.

Instead of dying, you simply choose to stop moving your body. You decide to occupy alternate structures of metaphysical space instead & we, at first, are understandably confused. One night, you take the form of rainbow dots scattered and sparkling on our ceiling. You seem to be able to be everywhere at once. After a while, we don't know what to do with your body, which is still breathing beneath a willow tree near the Goodwill. You become more and more elusive, sublime. At one point, in the final days before you enter some undetectable sphere and completely disappear, you attempt to show me a section of multidimensional activity. "Watch how all the realities intermingle!" you say. "Look at the way they merge and coalesce!" But it is too much for me. My own embodiment isn't ready.

Instead of dying, we go back in time, and I get to take away all the pain I caused you. Instead of dying, we go back in time, and I am allowed, somehow, to see myself causing you pain, and stop it. Instead of dying inside, you aren't dying inside. I get to say I am sorry and then even before I get to say I'm sorry, I get to prevent doing the things for which I am apologizing. For ignoring you, for teasing you in front of your friends, for trapping you, little brother, in a kennel once, in the basement several times, in headlocks and sleeper holds, in confusion, in all the ways those in power trap the weak. Instead of dying, you get to be free of the worst parts of me.

Instead of dying, you join a dogsledding team in Quebec. Each September you set off—a red stocking cap on your choppy hair, boots whacking the pineboard planks of the sled—into the brisk and opulent distance. Returning every four months, you bring us wood carvings of gnomes and rhizomes, geodes, crystals and maple sugar treats. Your beard becomes a sketchy palimpsest of your transformation. The terrible clawing pain that had once dug itself into your back now begins to quiet itself, slowly, until one morning, midway through your spring season, you wake up to find all of that endless, draining, life-defeating pain is gone. Gone. You pull your overalls up, cautiously, and then set out into what we will all look back on as the beginning of your relief. Letters from you smell like wood smoke, sprinkling salt on my desk as I open them one by one, and read.

Acknowledgments

Thank you, Susan Howe, for selecting this book. I will forever be star-struck by your consideration and in awe of your choice. Thank you to the Center for Literary Publishing, Colorado State University, and *Colorado Review,* with special thanks to Stephanie G'Schwind, Zach Yanowitz, Chelsea Hansen, and Sam Killmeyer for your careful review and editing, as well as your kindness. You have led me through the process with such grace and skill.

I am grateful to Candida Pagan at Digraph Press for fostering and publishing the poems contained in Section Four: "Ptolemy," "Aristotle," "Nicolaus Copernicus," "Tycho Brahe," "Johannes Kepler," "Galileo Galilei," "Isaac Newton," and "Eighth Heaven." These first appeared in "The Eccentricity Is Zero," a fine press artists book by Digraph Press in 2014. And thank you to Sarah Dodson and Joel Craig for publishing "Nicolaus Copernicus," "Galileo Galilei," "Tycho Brahe," and "Johannes Kepler" in *Make Magazine* #16, 2016.

My appreciation extends to the Denver Victim Compensation Program, for providing my family with such valuable assistance and support after the death of my brother; at a time when we needed so much care, the program was there to help.

I am thankful for support from the Sustainable Arts Foundation Award, which allowed me the time and resources needed to compose, edit, and complete this book. The benefits of SAF's mission are immeasurable.

Deep gratitude to the following people whose own work inspired these poems, or whose support nurtured them into being: Kiki Petrosino, Amy Shearn, Zach Savich, Caryl Pagel, Danny Khalastchi, Lynne Nugent, Dan Beachy-Quick, Suzanne Buffam, Robyn Schiff, Nick Twemlow, Camille Dungy, Amy Margolis, Mark Leidner, Kelly Smith, Jesse Nathan, Christopher Merrill, Dean Young, Jonathan Galassi, and Shane McCrae.

As always, my full & infinite love to family near and far; to Kitty and Eddie, my animal family; and to Ben Fortune and Ellie Fortune, my people.

This book is set in Sabon and Poplar
by The Center for Literary Publishing
at Colorado State University.

Copyediting by Zach Yanowitz.
Proofreading by Chelsea Hansen.
Book design and typesetting by Stephanie G'Schwind.
Cover design by Sam Killmeyer.
Cover illustration by Lauren Haldeman.
Printing by BookMobile.